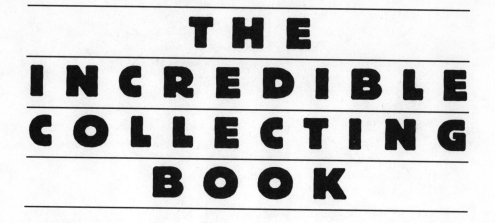

KidCollectors

THE INCREDIBLE COLLECTING BOOK

Kid Collectors

THE INCREDIBLE COLLECTING BOOK

Written by K. D. Kuch
Illustrated by Mike Moran

LOWELL HOUSE JUVENILE

LOS ANGELES

CONTEMPORARY BOOKS

CHICAGO

My special thanks to the 6th grade English teachers and students at Bangor Junior High. Your ideas, suggestions, and especially your KidCollections were a great inspiration.

To my fellow flying pig collectors—keep believing in the impossible!

—K. D. K.

Reviewed and endorsed by Steve Ellingboe,
editor of *Today's Collector* magazine

Publisher: Jack Artenstein
Director of Publishing Services: Rena Copperman
Executive Managing Editor, Juvenile: Brenda Pope-Ostrow
Editor in Chief, Juvenile: Amy Downing
Cover Photographs: Tony David Photography
Typesetting and Design: Carolyn Wendt

Library of Congress Catalog Card Number: 97-73967

ISBN: 1-56565-732-2

Lowell House books can be purchased at special discounts when ordered in bulk for premiums and special sales. Contact Department TC at the following address:

Lowell House Juvenile
2020 Avenue of the Stars, Suite 300
Los Angeles, CA 90067

Manufactured in the United States of America

10 9 8 7 6 5 4 3 2 1

CONTENTS

FROM ORDINARY KID TO INCREDIBLE COLLECTOR

D o you have baseball cards packed in shoe boxes under your bed? Do stuffed animals fill every nook and cranny of your bedroom? Do you have one dresser drawer loaded with key chains?

If you do, don't think of your stuff as . . . well, just stuff! Instead, think of yourself as a collector, with your stuff as the beginning of an incredible collection. All you need to make it true is a little planning, organizing, and maintenance of your collection.

You're not alone, either. According to Gale Research, a Detroit, Michigan, research firm, Americans spend over $5 billion a year for their collections. And they're not just spending their money on expensive, one-of-a-kind items, such as antique dolls or artwork. Collections can be made up of ordinary items, such as:

- old hats
- marbles
- newspapers
- bookmarks
- pigs
- salt and pepper shakers
- bottles
- baskets

Each collection is unique to its owner. It may have a special meaning, like keepsakes from trips. Or the collection may just be something the owner likes, such as cow figures.

You can start a collection no matter how much money you have to spend or where you live. A lot of people—kids included—put together terrific collections with things that are free or that cost very little. And this book will help you do it!

Whether you're already a collector or you want to be, *The Incredible Collecting Book* will help you plan, organize, and maintain your own collection. Here you'll find lots of fun and creative ideas to make collecting a special part of your life.

So what are you waiting for? Start collecting!

COLLECTING STATS

Collecting is becoming one of America's favorite pastimes, according to a 1996 survey sponsored by Enesco Corporation, a manufacturer of collectibles. At least 55 percent of the people responding to the survey reported collecting as their hobby. They also found that almost 29 percent of the adults surveyed collected with their children.

THE FUN OF COLLECTING

"I started collecting skeleton keys when I was eight. I got started when I saw a movie and it had a really neat skeleton key in it. I wondered how many of that kind of key I could find. I'm hoping to have at least a hundred keys soon."

Johanna, age 12

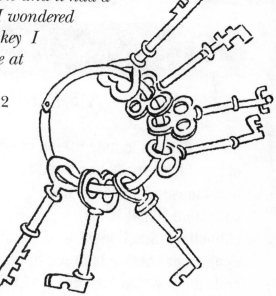

Y ou probably already know someone who has a collection. Perhaps your mom collects china teacups, or your dad's workshop is filled with antique tools. Maybe your big brother has a collection of coins, and your best friend is bonkers over Beanie Babies™ (those ultrapopular bean-stuffed critters). The big question is, why collect?

KIDCOLLECTOR TIP #1

Collect what you like. Don't worry about what everyone else is collecting or whether your collection will go up in value. If you spend too much time agonizing over the value of your collectible, you won't be able to enjoy it now.

● **Collecting can be enjoyed by anyone.** Kids do it and so do grandparents—no matter what your age or interest, there is a collection waiting for you. Once you decide what that collection is, you will spend many enjoyable hours with your favorite objects.

● **Collecting sharpens your skills.** Researching and hunting for items to add to your collection are the first skills you will develop. Once your collection is started, you will also work on other skills, such as

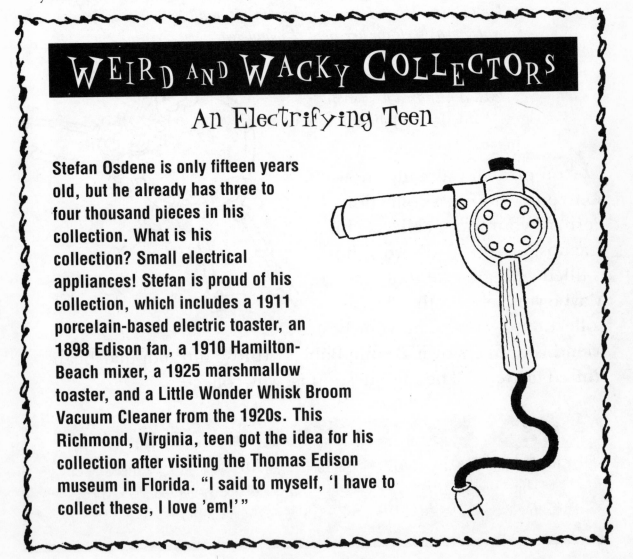

WEIRD AND WACKY COLLECTORS

An Electrifying Teen

Stefan Osdene is only fifteen years old, but he already has three to four thousand pieces in his collection. What is his collection? Small electrical appliances! Stefan is proud of his collection, which includes a 1911 porcelain-based electric toaster, an 1898 Edison fan, a 1910 Hamilton-Beach mixer, a 1925 marshmallow toaster, and a Little Wonder Whisk Broom Vacuum Cleaner from the 1920s. This Richmond, Virginia, teen got the idea for his collection after visiting the Thomas Edison museum in Florida. "I said to myself, 'I have to collect these, I love 'em!'"

classification, categorization, and even math. Just because you're learning, don't think you won't have a lot of fun, too. Say you decide to collect rocks. First you need to identify the rocks you find. Then you need to label and display them. You might even be curious about the role of rocks in history, like how the Pyramids were built. Who knows, your collecting could evolve into types of stones used for building, or rocks from historical sites. How much do you think a piece of the Berlin Wall is worth?

My KidCollection

"I collect baseball cards. I received a big box of cards for Christmas when I was six years old. Now I buy more cards at stores and I trade with my friends. If you collect, you should get a magazine that tells the prices of your cards so you know what to trade. You'll find lots of them at stores, especially sports card shops. You don't want to trade a $25 card for a $1 card."

JEFF, AGE 11

- **Collecting is a cool way to make new friends.** Collecting is a fun free-time activity you can share with other people. You'll find other collectors through collector's clubs, shows, and even the Internet. But you don't have to belong to any special organization or club to meet other collectors. Just start talking about your new collection. You will find others who are interested—maybe even kids at your school who collect the same thing.

- **Collecting is affordable.** Collectibles come in all shapes, sizes, and prices. Many things are available for no money at all. With a little creativity you can come up with your own alternatives to expensive collectibles. High-priced items, such as antique coins, may attract adults, but you can start—and enjoy just as much—your own penny collection.

● **Collecting can be an investment.** Imagine a baseball card selling for close to half a million dollars. Deals like that do happen, but not very often. Still, that's one reason a lot of people like to collect. They hope to strike it rich, too. When there are more collectors than pieces to be collected, prices shoot up.

Sports cards are a good example. For years adults and children collected them without spending a lot of money. Then some collectors wanted to add cards of early baseball players to their collections. But there weren't as many of those cards

My KidCollection

"I collect glass statues. I started my collection when I went to Kings Island two years ago and bought a glass swan. I was nine years old at the time. I look for them wherever I go, especially in gift shops."

ELIZABETH, AGE 11

INVESTING IN YOUR COLLECTION

Stories about people who buy a collectible for a little money, then turn around and sell it for a bundle sound really cool. But that doesn't usually happen. Even professional dealers—people who buy and sell collectibles for a living—realize that. They know it takes time for a collectible to increase in value. Furthermore, many factors can affect its worth, such as how rare the collectible is and what condition it is in. If you decide to start and maintain a collection as an investment, get your parents involved. Their guidance and advice will help you make the right decisions.

available anymore. Suddenly, those "rare" cards became very expensive, too expensive for the average collector. While it may be nice to dream of making profits, the truth is, no one knows which collectibles will go up in value.

KIDCOLLECTOR TIP #2

Get your whole family involved in collecting. Pick something everyone likes, for instance, rock collecting. Then, as a family, learn about your new hobby and spend time together gathering rocks for your collection. Work together to create an interesting display.

CHOOSING WHAT TO COLLECT

"I collect sand whenever we go on a trip. I've got some from White Sands Monument in New Mexico, beaches in California, and some from a trip to Lake Michigan last summer. I put them in old bottles I find at garage sales and line them up on my window."

Mike, age 14

You might think choosing something to collect is easy. Well, not always. There are so many things to choose from—stamps, books, dolls, baseball cards, arrowheads, and marbles, to name a few. Determining what you should collect is a process of trial and error. It's based on your personality, as well as your likes and dislikes. Read on for some ideas to help you narrow down the possibilities.

WHAT CAN BE A COLLECTIBLE?

The answer is anything. Think of an object and someone probably collects it. Some of the most fun collections are the most unusual—soda pop cans, items advertising characters like the Campbell's® Soup Kids, bookmarks, calendars, buttons, and even small kitchen appliances are stuff people collect. If you haven't decided what to collect yet, take a look at how some people started their favorite collections.

A Favorite Thing

Sometimes people don't even realize they already have a collection started. Does this sound familiar? As long as you can remember, you have loved sunflowers. Your bedspread has huge sunflowers, your bedroom walls have stenciled sunflowers, even your school folders have little sunflowers on them. With this favorite theme you have the start of a collection. The only difference is that you should record what you receive, and you may need to take better care of the items.

A Family Heirloom

A lot of collections start because an older family member hands down his or her collection to a younger member of the family. Maybe your dad collected baseball cards and he wants to share his interest with you. Or perhaps your grandmother wants to give you her collection of old buttons. Continuing the collection gives you the opportunity to carry on a family tradition, as well as share a rewarding hobby with someone you love.

A Souvenir

When you travel, do you always buy something to remember where you've been? Collecting souvenirs—like maps, collector pins, cups, and postcards—is an easy way to start a collection. And it's a fun way to remember special trips.

WEIRD AND WACKY COLLECTORS

When One Is Not Enough

What happens when you have so many collections you can't find a place to put them all? You write a book! That's what Mary Randolph Carter did. She's the author of *American Junk* (1994, Studio) and *American Junk: How to Hunt For, Haggle Over, Rescue and Transform America's Forgotten Treasures* (1997, Penguin USA). For this self-proclaimed "passionate junker" the collecting bug struck early. And hard! As a child, she had her own special corner of the family attic devoted to her collections—everything from odd bits of fabric and hardware to tins and pottery. "I've never collected anything just because it's valuable," Mary has said. By the time Mary reached junior high school, her collections and displays moved downstairs. She strung old fishing net on her walls and used it to hang up her weird collections. She knew she was different from her friends, but that didn't matter because her collections meant something to her. She said, "Certain things just clutch at my heart."

A Special Interest

Do you have a special subject you like in school? Maybe you're the only person you know who loves studying rocks and minerals in science class. If so, you should transfer your interest in geology (the study of rocks and minerals) to a rocks and minerals collection. A special interest is a natural starting point. If you like cooking, then collect cookbooks. If you love spending time at the beach, collect shells. Collections based on an interest are a fun way to keep learning.

A Favorite Theme

If collecting one kind of object seems boring, think about collecting items that focus on one central idea, such as a time period or a favorite TV show.

My KidCollection

"I collect dice. I started when I found some dice in a magic trick when I was ten years old. I look for different-colored ones at hobby stores and old dice at flea markets. Dice are very easy to collect and you can keep them in a shoe box. If you have a big collection, you can make up games of your own."

ANDREW, AGE 11

KIDCOLLECTOR TIP #3

Old Pez dispensers are really hot collectibles at the moment. A 1976 Daniel Boone dispenser can cost $200, and a Tinkerbell from the 1960s runs $75. You don't have to pay those high prices to start a collection. New Pez dispensers and candy cost under $2. Eat the candy now and save the dispenser for your collection.

The goal is to collect all sorts of different objects that relate to that one theme. Here are some ideas:

▲ **TV show or movie:** Start a collection based on a favorite show or movie. Begin your collection with some videos. Many older and even some new shows can be found on video. If that's not possible, tape your favorite show if you have a video recorder. Then look for other items to add to your collection. Popular movies and television shows, such as *Batman* or *Star Trek*, have lots of stuff. You'll find toy figures, T-shirts, comic books, posters, and even trading cards.

▲ **Hometown collection:** Be proud of your hometown and start a collection. Gift stores might carry T-shirts and cups displaying your town's name. The same goes for postcards. Start a scrapbook and look for old photographs that show your hometown's history and how it has developed. Check with older relatives who may have old photographs from when they were growing up.

My KidCollection

"I have two collections, rocks and Baby-Sitters Club books. I first started collecting rocks when I was eight—that's my outside collection. The books are my inside collection. I mostly buy those at the stores or get them as gifts."

LEIGH, AGE 11

K I D C O L L E C T O R   T I P   #4

Don't be upset if you get another of the same toy the next time you buy your favorite fast-food meal. It's the best thing that could happen. Put one toy in your collection (make sure to keep it in its original packaging) and use the extra toy to play with or trade with friends.

WEIRD AND WACKY COLLECTORS

From Candy to Cash

It's hard to believe, but candy you can buy now might be worth hundreds of dollars in the future. Just look at David Welch, a collector who buys and sells Pez* candy dispensers, the plastic candy dispensers in the shape of cartoon characters. In 1989, David bought 115 Pez dispensers at an antique show for $1,000. He remembered the candy as a kid and had a "hunch" it would be worth something. Boy, was he right. Almost immediately, he turned around and sold those 115, making a $5,000 profit! Most turned out to be rare and valuable items that other Pez collectors wanted. Before he sold the Pez dispensers, people thought David was nuts. "I'm not so sure I'm not crazy either," said this "Pezzimist" (as some Pez collectors call themselves). The "hunch" has now turned into a full-time Pez career. Not only does David continue to buy and sell Pez dispensers, he's also authored books about the Pez collecting craze—*A Pictorial Guide to Plastic Candy Dispensers* (1991) and *Collecting Pez* (1996), both published by Bubba Scrubba.

The candy originated in Austria in 1927. Pez is a shortened form of the German word Pfefferminz, *which means "peppermint."*

▲ **Make it Toony:** From Mickey Mouse to Bugs Bunny, cartoon characters are everywhere and on all types of merchandise. You can find cartoon character toys, T-shirts, and even drinking glasses. Also check out cereal boxes with cartoon characters on the front, comic strips in the newspaper, and special giveaways at your local fast-food restaurants.

My KidCollection

"I collect trolls. When I was getting my ears pierced, I had to hold on to something. I picked up a troll doll from the counter. That's when I knew I wanted to collect troll dolls. They're special."

GINA, AGE 11

WOULD YOU LIKE A COLLECTIBLE WITH YOUR FRIES?

So, you think people go to McDonald's for the Big Macs? Wrong. At least for some collectors, who are drawn to the popular fast-food chains for the toy giveaways inside Happy Meals. Fast-food premiums have been popular collectibles since they were first introduced by McDonald's in 1977. But nothing has beat the premium craze for the miniature version of Beanie Babies, the popular, cuddly bean-stuffed animals. The Beanie Babies giveaway was scheduled to run for three weeks in April 1997. Within the first week McDonald's franchises across the country reported they were completely out of stock! Though it may take years, some classic Happy Meals toys fetch big bucks, selling for up to eighty times their value. McDonald's isn't the only fast-food chain giving away toys with their meals. Most major fast-food chains also include toys with the purchase of a child's meal.

21

THE CHOICE IS YOURS – A COLLECTOR'S QUIZ

Don't worry, there's no grading on this quiz. These questions will get you thinking about the collectible category that's right for you. Pull out a pencil and paper, then write down your answers to each of the following questions.

1. What are my favorite things?

Make a list of your favorites from the following categories. After you've finished your list, compare your answers to what you see in your own room. Anything worth collecting? If you like it, then it is!

What or who is your favorite:

- color
- shape
- animal
- sport
- game

- TV show or movie
- holiday
- sports hero
- movie or television star

2. Do I want a traditional collection or one that's unique?

Do you like being a little different from everyone else? Or is it more important to you to be part of the crowd?

3. How much money can I spend on my collection?

How will you pay for your collection? Do you get an allowance? Or will you have to do extra chores around the house to earn money? The biggest question of all is, how much of your money will you want to set aside for your collection?

4. Do I want to collect as an investment?

Do you hope to sell your collection for a profit someday?

5. How much time can I give up for collecting?

Do you have lots of after-school activities, such as music classes or sports, that occupy your time?

6. Do I have the space for a collection?

Do you intend to display your collection?

What your answers mean:

1. If you say your favorite colors are red, white, and blue, and those are the primary colors in your room, you might want to collect American flags. Or if you answer that basketball is your favorite sport, and a basketball hoop is a permanent fixture in your room, it's a slam dunk you'll want to collect basketball memorabilia.

2. The more traditional the collection—say stamps, dolls, coins, or sports cards—the easier it will be to find others who collect.

3. Collecting can be like eating potato chips—you can't eat just one. It's easy to want everything you see and end up spending too much money. You'll have to decide how much money you can spend. Most collectors set a limit for themselves. So if you're short on cash, you may have to find ways to earn money for your collection.

COLLECTING THE FORCE

Who would think that after twenty years collectors would still be crazy for *Star Wars* characters? It's true, the *Star Wars* trilogy—*Star Wars, The Empire Strikes Back,* and *Return of the Jedi*—made a huge comeback on the twentieth anniversary. You can find all-new toy figures of the characters in your local stores or even as fast-food premiums. But the hottest of all the characters isn't Luke, Han, Princess Leia, or Darth Vader. It's Boba Fett, the cosmic bounty hunter. If you blinked during the movies, you may have missed him. Boba Fett only appeared for about eight minutes on screen. Now toy figures based on that character outsell all the others—some people have paid up to $2,500 to own a Boba Fett.

4. Some people start collections so they can sell them later. These people speculate that a collectible today will be worth more money in the future. Sometimes it works out, sometimes it doesn't. No one knows how long it will take for a collectible to increase in value. If you decide to sell collectibles, proceed slowly and don't expect to make piles of money.

5. The amount of time you spend on your collection is up to you. Some people spend very little time. Others put a great deal of effort into finding, organizing, and displaying their collections. That can cut into your free time, so think carefully. Are you willing to spend weeks of Saturday afternoons searching for those perfect pieces to add to your collection?

6. Collections can take up a lot of space. Do you have room for extra bookcases and shelves in your room? If you share a room with your brother, how will he feel about your collection spilling over into his side of the room? If space is a consideration, think small. A patch, pin, or autograph collection will take up less space than toy trains.

24

TAKE A PEEK IN THE NATION'S ATTIC

Abraham Lincoln's hat, the Wright brothers' biplane, Kermit the Frog, the ruby slippers worn by Judy Garland in *The Wizard of Oz,* and the leather jacket and suede fedora worn by Harrison Ford in the *Indiana Jones* movies—these items may not sound like things you have in your attic, but you can find them at the Smithsonian Institution's museums in Washington, D.C.

The Smithsonian Institution is called the "nation's attic" because it has some of the biggest and best scientific and cultural collections to be found. Started in 1846, the Smithsonian Institution is a complex of fourteen museums sponsored by the U.S. government. These include The National Air and Space Museum, the Freer Gallery of Art, the National Portrait Gallery, and the National Museum of American Art. But you don't have to go all the way to Washington, D.C., to see any of these wonderful collections. Each year the Smithsonian sponsors traveling exhibits that are presented in different cities around the country. For current information on where and when exhibits are planned, call the Smithsonian at 1-800-913-TOUR, or for the entire list of locations, visit the Smithsonian's Home Page on the World Wide Web (http://www.si.edu). Maybe one of the more than 140 million artifacts in the Smithsonian Institution's museums will inspire you to start a new collection.

WHAT KIND OF COLLECTOR ARE YOU?

All types of people collect. Often a collection will reflect something about its owner. Look over the various types of collectors and see which category you fall into. Knowing that may help you figure out what to collect.

● **The Champion Collector** likes to collect objects revolving around a hero, such as an undefeated sports team, a sports star, or a popular movie actor. Baseball cards of popular sports stars and autographs from famous people are the most typical collections.

● **The Emotional Collector** likes to collect things that have a special meaning, or represent a sentimental occasion. If you fall into this category, you might want to collect old Valentines, postcards, or travel souvenirs.

● **The Eccentric Collector** likes things that are unique. If no one else collects this object, then this collector will! Collecting sand or saving bricks from demolished buildings might be just the thing for this collector.

● **The Classic Collector** likes traditional collections that have been around for a long time. Stamps and coins are just what this collector is looking for.

SHE'S A REAL DOLL

Would you believe a Barbie™ doll collecting dust in the bottom of your closet is one of today's hottest collectibles? It might be true if you own a doll that Barbie collectors want. Barbie enthusiasts (called Barbiephiles) search everywhere for their favorites—especially a Barbie doll in perfect condition, still in the original box and plastic wrapping. The Barbie doll was introduced in 1959 at a New York toy fair and was named after the inventor's own daughter. The old, hard-to-find Barbie dolls are not the only hot collectibles. New, limited edition, collector Barbie dolls in exquisite gowns can cost close to $200. Barbiephiles can also choose from among more than 200 accessories and a wardrobe that grows by 100 outfits a year. So if you're thinking of throwing away those old Barbie dolls . . . stop! You might have the beginning of a hot new collection.

- **The Everything Collector** doesn't have a special focus. Everything appeals to this person. There are no rules that say you can collect only one category. In fact, lots of collectors have five or six (or more) collections.

My KidCollection

"I collect Barbie dolls and Barbie stuff. My collection got started when my mom gave me a Barbie doll and a couch when I was two years old. I've been collecting for nine years now. My dad even made me a house for my Barbie collection."

AMBER, AGE 11

27

THE TOP TEN THINGS TO COLLECT

"I like to collect coins from different countries. My cousins in Canada send me coins. And if anyone I know is going on a trip, I ask them to bring me back a coin. My best find was three coins from Poland that I found at a garage sale."

Eric, age 11

Some categories of collecting stand out from the rest. These are the always-popular, everyone-loves-them, been-around-for-years collections. Within these "classic" categories you will find countless collectibles, usually at reasonable prices. You'll also find a lot of other collectors like yourself. Collectibles fads come and go, but you won't go wrong with these top ten "classics."

1. TRADING CARDS

Facts

A trading card is a 2½" x 3½" card with a photo of a hero on the front and fun stats on the back. Sports dominate the trading card market—25 million people collect only sports cards! But these days you can find more than just sports stars on trading cards. Movie characters, such as Batman and Robin, are popular figures on trading cards, too.

A Little History

Trading cards originated in the mid-1800s. Tobacco companies were among the first to use trading cards as a way to advertise their products. The modern age of trading cards began in 1951, when the Topps Chewing Gum Company began including baseball cards with their product.

Where to Find

The easiest way to start card collecting is at your local grocery store or bookstore. Even discount stores such as Target and Wal-Mart carry packs of cards. Some cards are given away for advertising and have been included with everything from cereal boxes to dog food. Old and rare cards are sold through dealers or other collectors.

What It Will Cost

New packages of cards (five to ten per pack) cost around $2. Some packs still come with a piece of gum inside. Older and hard-to-come-by cards can cost hundreds of dollars.

Tips

Try collecting cards for all the members of your favorite team. Start collecting early because cards can become scarce, especially if the team is on a winning streak. Once you have done that, then try to collect cards for a particular year. To protect your cards, put them in special plastic storage sheets sold at hobby shops.

For More Info

Check your library for a copy of *Sports Cards Magazine,* or the *Official Price Guide for Baseball Cards* (House of Collectibles Publishing) by Dr. James Beckett, which has current prices of baseball cards and is updated regularly.

2. STAMPS

Facts

According to the American Philatelic Society, a national organization for stamp collectors, up to 10 million people collect stamps. The typical stamp collector starts at eight years old and continues the hobby for his or her lifetime.

A Little History

The first collector was a little girl. The story goes that in 1841 the British newspaper *The Times* printed a letter asking their readers to send postage stamps to a young girl who was collecting them. No one knows who that girl was, but there have been many famous collectors since. Franklin D. Roosevelt, thirty-second president of the United States, was a subject on a stamp, but he was also a lifelong stamp collector. It was a form of relaxation for President Roosevelt, who tried to put some time into his collection each day.

Where to Find

The U.S. Postal Service prints thirty to fifty new commemorative stamps each year. These stamps can honor different people or characters, such as Bugs Bunny or Elvis Presley. Some stamps display a subject of interest, like famous artwork or wildlife. The best way to start your collection is at the Post Office. The Postal Service has free information packets and even a Web site with loads of cool news (http://www.stampsonline.com). Older stamps can be found at specialty shops or through other collectors. Check the Yellow Pages in your phone book under *Stamps for Collectors*.

What It Will Cost

When buying new issues of stamps, you will pay the face value—that is, a 32-cent stamp will cost 32 cents. But older, rare, or special stamps can run into hundreds of dollars.

Tips

Some stamp hobbyists collect whatever stamps strike their fancy, while others like to specialize. People often collect stamps that are from certain countries, feature particular topics, or have errors. One way of keeping costs down is to ask out-of-town family members and friends to send you letters and postcards. You can then save the stamps for your collection.

For More Info

The American Philatelic Society is a national organization for stamp collectors. Many magazines and newsletters on the subject,

such as *Stamp Collector* and *Linn's Stamp News,* may be found at your local library.

You can write to the American Philatelic Society at:

American Philatelic Society
P.O. Box 8000
State College, PA 16803

3. ROCKS

Facts

Rocks are among the easiest and cheapest items to collect. Rocks can be found almost everywhere, even in your own backyard. You can begin collecting by simply bending over and picking up a rock that catches your eye. You can collect rocks for their size, color, or mineral value. You can also look for fossils in rocks.

A Little History

Rocks are usually classified as three main types: igneous, sedimentary, and metamorphic. Igneous rocks form within the earth from the crystallization of cooled molten rock material, or magma. Sedimentary rocks form at the bottom of lakes and oceans from minerals and grains of other rocks. Metamorphic rocks have been altered into new states by extreme pressure, temperature, or water.

Where to Find

Rocks can be found anywhere. Start by searching for rocks unique to your area. Rock and mineral shops sell very rare and special rocks from around the world. Check your phone book for listings under *Rock Shops.*

What It Will Cost

Finding rocks in your own area is the easiest way to keep costs down. Even if your rocks cost nothing, you can still spend money on the extras. Some rock collectors (or "rock hounds," as they're sometimes called) like to polish their rocks. A rock polishing machine can be found at a hobby store for $20 and up. And if you're looking for a special type of rock, you may have to search it out in a rock store.

Tips

Display your rocks on trays. Make a card for each rock describing where and when you found it and what kind of rock it is.

For More Info

Your local library should have books on rocks and rock collecting to help you. While you're there, also check to see if they have *Rocks and Minerals Magazine* or *American Mineralogist,* a bimonthly publication of the Mineralogical Society of America. Write to them at:

Mineralogical Society of America
1625 Eye St., NW, Suite 414
Washington, DC 20006

4. DOLLS AND STUFFED ANIMALS

Facts

Doll and stuffed animal collecting is a popular pastime. Some of the most popular items to collect are antique dolls (those that are more than 100 years old), Madame Alexander dolls (exquisitely costumed designer dolls made especially for collectors), and Barbie dolls. Teddy Bears are the all-time favorite stuffed animal to collect. Antique bears,

dressed-up bears, even bears designed especially for collectors (called collector teddy bears), are always popular. Right now the hottest stuffed animals around are the Beanie Babies.

A Little History

Collecting dolls is only the beginning for some collectors. For some, accessories are just as important. The best-dressed doll—and teddy bear—may have a whole closet full of outfits. Dollhouses, furniture, and even books are important accessories. The Raggedy Ann and Andy dolls are a

THE TEDDY BEAR RALLY

Teddy Bears are so popular there's even a Teddy Bear Rally held in Amherst, Massachusetts, every year. It's true! Each summer for the past fifteen years people and their bears have come from all over the country to participate. Approximately 25,000 people attend the festivities, which include a parade, a picnic for children and their bears, and a teddy bear hospital where teddies get "beary" good treatment. For more information, call the Amherst Chamber of Commerce at (413) 253-0700. (Be sure to get a parent's permission before calling.)

perfect example. The dolls were originally created to help sell the stories written by Johnny Gruelle, starting with the first book, *Raggedy Ann Stories,* in 1918. Although the Raggedy Ann books were successful, the dolls became more popular.

Where to Find

Collector dolls and teddy bears are sold by specialty stores, through mail-order catalogs, or by other collectors. Some toy stores and gift shops carry these dolls, too.

My KidCollection

"I like to collect porcelain dolls. I got started when I was about four years old and my mother gave me a doll for Christmas. My mom collects dolls, too. They're kind of expensive, so we don't have a lot, yet."

JENNIFER, AGE 12

EVEN THE FAMOUS COLLECT

What do talk-show host and actress Rosie O'Donnell and Olympic gold medalist Jackie Joyner-Kersee have in common? They both collect dolls. Jackie started out by collecting celebrity dolls, then she decided to make Barbie dolls her main focus. She enjoys searching out Barbie dolls whenever she travels to another country. Rosie, on the other hand, doesn't limit her collection to dolls. Yes, she has those, including a Chatty Cathy doll from the 1960s and a Mrs. Beasley doll from *Family Affair* (a 1970s TV show). But it's the 2,500 McDonald's Happy Meal toys that dominate her collection. Rosie started collecting them in the 1980s when she toured the country as a stand-up comic.

What It Will Cost

Collector dolls and teddy bears can be very expensive. A new Madame Alexander doll can sell for $75, and older dolls are worth several hundred dollars. On the other end of the scale, new Beanie Babies sell for around $6.

Tips

It's true that some dolls and stuffed animals are very expensive, but don't let that stop you from starting a collection. Look for dolls and stuffed animals you like and can afford at garage sales and flea markets.

For More Info

Doll Values: Antique to Modern (1997, Collector Books) by Patsy Moyer is a source book filled with information on the ever-changing doll market. Also check your local library's magazine section for *Dolls—The Collector's Magazine,* published monthly.

5. SPORTS MEMORABILIA

Facts

Besides trading cards, there's a whole category of collectibles associated with professional sports teams. Tickets, pins, balls, clothing, and programs are just the start. A piece of memorabilia becomes more valuable when it is autographed by a sports celebrity.

A Little History

Many collectors turned to collecting sports memorabilia as the prices of trading cards went up. Still, some prices of sports memorabilia are climbing, too, especially for anything autographed. Some people like to collect memorabilia associated with a favorite team, like tickets or programs from sporting events they attend. Others collect just one type of item, like autographed baseballs.

Where to Find

Sports memorabilia can be found in many places. Check out big sports equipment stores, trading card shops, or discount and department stores. Other collectors are also good sources. Baseball card and sports memorabilia shows are held in major cities across the country.

What It Will Cost

High prices for some memorabilia—especially signed balls and uniforms—can put a dent in a collector's pocket. But not all sports memorabilia is expensive, such as a season schedule, which is a listing of a team's games for the season. Advertisers print and distribute thousands of copies of these in stores—from your local party store to your favorite sports shop. The cost of these schedules? They're free!

Tips

If your budget is tight, you can save newspaper stories about your favorite teams. Cut out the articles and paste them into a scrapbook. Remember to include photographs.

For More Info

To find out what sports memorabilia people are collecting and what current prices are, look for this book at your local library: *Malloy's Sports Collectibles Value Guide: Up-To-Date Prices for Noncard Sports Memorabilia* (1993, Wallace-Homestead Books) by Roderick A. Malloy.

A COLLECTOR'S GLOSSARY

Two terms you will see a lot in this book are *flea market* and *swap meet*. You may already know what these terms mean and may have attended one of these events. They are big, open-air markets with individual vendors selling all kinds of things, from pictures to hang on the wall to pitchers used to serve lemonade.

6. AUTOGRAPHS

Facts

According to the Universal Autograph Collectors Club, about two million people collect autographs. Many people collect signatures from baseball players (especially members of the Baseball Hall of Fame), movie stars

(particularly those who win Academy Awards), and American politicians (primarily presidents). While these autographs are the most valuable, it's fun to collect autographs from people who are not famous, too. Old letters and papers are also collected for their historical importance.

A Little History

Autograph collecting is one of the world's oldest hobbies. One of the first philographers (a name given to autograph collectors) was a Roman statesman named Cicero. He collected letters written by famous people

living in Rome. His most prized signature was on a letter written to him by the Emperor Julius Caesar!

Where to Find

Most autographs are sold by dealers or other collectors. But some people are lucky enough to get autographs on their own.

What It Will Cost

Prices for autographs and signed documents can cost as little as five dollars or as much as thousands of dollars, depending on whose signature it is and the rarity of the signed document.

Tips

You can start collecting autographs without spending much. Write to famous people asking for their autographs. Not all celebrities will respond, but some will, if not with an actual autograph, then with a photograph or other information. Collect autographs of people with interesting signatures, or collect the autographs of your school's staff. Years from now you'll have fun looking back at all the signatures.

For More Info

If you're interested in what autographs are available and their current prices, check your library for a copy of *The Sanders Price Guide to Autographs* (1994, Alexander Books). You can also write to:

Universal Autograph Collectors Club
P.O. Box 467, Dept. JM
Rockville Centre, NY 11571

7. COINS

Facts

Why is coin collecting so popular? One reason is that it's easy to start—just reach into your pocket and pull out some change. Some of the pennies, nickels, and dimes of today can be worth several times their

value in the future. Many people collect rare and special issue coins (coins made to commemorate an event, such as the Olympics).

A Little History

A coin's worth is determined by its quality and how many of that type of coin are still in existence. One of the most valuable coins today is the 1913 Liberty head nickel because there are only five known to exist. Collectors also like to find uncirculated coins. Those are coins that have never been used.

Where to Find

Old and rare coins are sold by dealers and through other collectors. But you don't have to go far—or spend a lot of money—to find coins. Empty out your piggy bank and sort through any coins you have. Some may be brand-new coins, and others will be a few years old. Those coins can be the framework of a good collection.

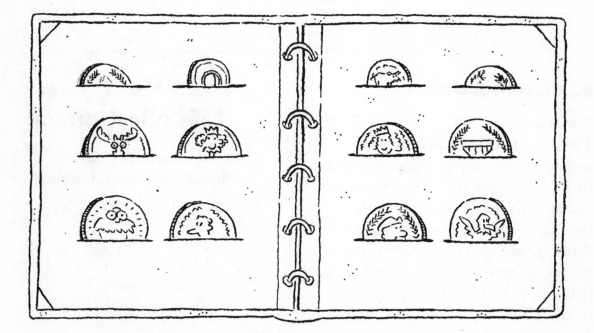

What It Will Cost

An old, rare coin in mint (perfect) condition can be very expensive. Even a tiny scratch on the surface takes away from the coin's value. It's better to start your collection with currently minted coins.

Tips

Whenever you have extra coins jingling in your pocket, throw them in a glass jar. When the jar gets full, dump the coins on a table and start to sort through them. Pick up the coins you want to add to your collection and spend the rest!

For More Info

The American Numismatic Association has a special program just for young people, and it's free. Also check to see if your local library has *Coins,* a monthly magazine for collectors that includes a calendar of coin shows. For more information on the American Numismatic Association, write to:

American Numismatic Association
542 Webster Ave.
New Rochelle, NY 10805

8. COMIC BOOKS

Facts

The first comic drawings appeared in newspapers over one hundred years ago. They were an instant hit. Ever since, people have cut out the comics from their newspapers and saved them. Those simple comic panels led to full comic books. The first comic book to sell on newsstands was *Famous Funnies* in 1934.

My KidCollection

"I love comic books. My collection started when my baby-sitter gave me some old comic books. I was about eight. I buy new ones from stores now."

PATRICK, AGE 12

A Little History

Today, over a hundred different titles are published every month. You can find funny comics based on popular television shows, such as *Pinky and the Brain* or *The Simpsons*. But the mainstay of the comic books are superheroes. Superman, Batman, and the X-Men are characters started in comic books that have had successful television series and movies. Many comic books are published as limited series that may only have one to six issues. These comic books can become more valuable almost immediately because of their limited supply.

Where to Find

Old and new comic books can be found in comic book shops. Popular titles from the large publishers (like Marvel and DC Comics) are sold in bookstores, grocery stores, and even your local convenience store. Comic books from smaller publishers, as well as older and rare comic books, can be found at your local comic book shop or purchased from other collectors.

What It Will Cost

New comic books cost about $2 to $3. The value of a comic book is usually determined by its condition and the number of copies available.

Tips

Comic books can be collected for the publisher (like Marvel or DC Comics), for characters (like Spiderman), or even for the artist or writer. The most important aspect of a collection is the physical

condition of the comic books. Comic book collectors take special care in storing and preserving their comics by putting them in special plastic sleeves that can be bought at comic book shops.

For More Info

Check out your favorite comic book store for *Comic Buyers Guide* and *Overstreet Comic Book Marketplace*. Both these price guides are packed with information on the most popular comic books, as well as the latest prices.

9. MODEL KITS

Facts

If you like to build things yourself, consider model kits. A kit comes with all the plastic parts you need to build a variety of models. Automobiles are usually associated with model kits. But you'll find all types of plastic models that come ready to build—trucks, planes, helicopters, even dinosaurs. Most collectors specialize in either assembled or unassembled models.

A Little History

Automobile model kits originated in England in the mid-1930s, but they really hit it big in the 1960s. The models were manufactured to look exactly like the real cars. The hoods of the cars even open to reveal perfect, tiny replicas of the real engines. Corvettes and muscle cars (powerful two-door sports coupes) from the 1960s and 1970s are among the most sought-after models.

Where to Find

Check out the hobby section of your favorite toy store or discount store like Wal-Mart. If you're looking for older, discontinued models, search out antique stores with a toy section, or flea markets.

What It Will Cost

New kits usually cost under $6. But older kits, still unassembled, can cost two to three times that.

Tips

If you decide to build any models, do a good job. The ones done well will be worth more to other collectors.

For More Info

Check your local library for *Model and Toy Collector*, a magazine covering toys and model kits.

10. TOYS

Facts

Action figures, building toys, vehicles, and games are just a few choices for toy collections. Lots of adults collect toys now because it reminds them of their youth. Collectors may stick to buying one type of toy, such as Matchbox cars, or they may collect items from a specific time period, such as toys from the 1950s.

WEIRD AND WACKY COLLECTORS

"WHAT Kind of Bag?"

Barf bags! Who would collect barf bags? Harry L. Rinker would. Mr. Rinker is a writer, editor, and collector to the extreme. In books, magazines, and as a guest on radio shows, he gives advice about collecting. In his 1987 book *Rinker on Collectibles,* he revealed his weird and wacky side. Mr. Rinker collects airplane barf bags—empty ones, of course. As with many collectors, he didn't purposefully set out to start a collection of barf bags. It happened when he asked a friend's daughter to pick up any items that contained the logo or name of the plane she was flying on. The airline was rumored to be going out of business, so he wanted to collect whatever he could before its demise. One of the articles he received was a barf bag. From that first bag a whole collection grew.

Where to Find

Check out the hobby section of your favorite toy store or discount store like Wal-Mart. If you're looking for older, discontinued models, search out antique stores with a toy section, or flea markets.

What It Will Cost

New kits usually cost under $6. But older kits, still unassembled, can cost two to three times that.

Tips

If you decide to build any models, do a good job. The ones done well will be worth more to other collectors.

For More Info

Check your local library for *Model and Toy Collector,* a magazine covering toys and model kits.

10. TOYS

Facts

Action figures, building toys, vehicles, and games are just a few choices for toy collections. Lots of adults collect toys now because it reminds them of their youth. Collectors may stick to buying one type of toy, such as Matchbox cars, or they may collect items from a specific time period, such as toys from the 1950s.

A Little History

In the toy market—both old and new—licensed characters (from other sources like TV shows, books, and movies) usually outsell generic toys. Toys based on licensed characters will probably hold their value better, too. Toys issued as limited editions generally increase in value as well.

Where to Find

Older toys can be found at antique stores, swap meets, flea markets, and rummage sales. For new toys in the original packaging, check the large toy stores and discount chains. Toys 'Я' Us, Target, Wal-Mart, and the like are good places to start.

What It Will Cost

Old toys in perfect condition can be worth a lot of money. The toy is worth more if it has been kept in its original box with the instructions.

Tips

Before you throw away any of your old toys, take a closer look. If the toy has all its pieces and is in good condition, store it in the attic or at the back of a closet for the future. Some of the most popular collectibles today are based on children's toys, and many of these are from the 1940s and 1950s. Here are some of today's most sought-after toys from the past:

- **GI Joes:** This action figure toy was first made in 1964. GI Joes from the 1960s to the early 1980s are the most desired.

- **Matchbox cars:** These tiny die-cast cars were first made in 1953.

- **Viewmasters:** These binocular-shaped plastic viewers let you insert a film disk and view 3-D images.

- **Hopalong Cassidy:** Hopalong Cassidy was a popular cowboy TV and movie character in the 1950s. His image was on everything from lunch boxes to toy pistols.

- **Roy Rogers:** He was a singing cowboy who starred in movies and on a television series with his real-life wife, Dale Evans. A variety of toys

appeared portraying their images, including toy guitars, holsters and pistols, and cowboy vests and hats.

- **Howdy Doody:** This puppet character was the star of his own TV show in the 1950s. There were many toys that carried the Howdy Doody image, but the most popular is the Howdy Doody doll.

- **Winky Dink:** He is a less known, but still popular animated TV character from the 1950s.

- **Lunch boxes:** School lunch boxes with famous TV, cartoon, and toy characters are the most popular.

- **Premiums from cereal boxes:** Prizes, such as rings or compasses, have been put in cereal boxes since the 1920s.

- *Star Wars* **items:** Action figures and other *Star Wars* toys from the first movie twenty years ago are the most desired.

My KidCollection

"My collection is postcards. I just started saving all the postcards in our house when I was about five years old. I have about 150 postcards from all over the world. Friends and family send them to me whenever they're on vacation. I keep all my postcards in a photo album. I write who each one is from next to it in the book."

ARIEL, AGE 11

For More Info

Your library may have lots of books on various types of toy collecting. If you're interested in current prices for old toys, check for a copy of the *1998 Toys and Prices* (Krause Publication), a price guide with updated information for toys from the 1840s to the present.

WEIRD AND WACKY COLLECTORS

"WHAT Kind of Bag?"

Barf bags! Who would collect barf bags? Harry L. Rinker would. Mr. Rinker is a writer, editor, and collector to the extreme. In books, magazines, and as a guest on radio shows, he gives advice about collecting. In his 1987 book *Rinker on Collectibles,* he revealed his weird and wacky side. Mr. Rinker collects airplane barf bags—empty ones, of course. As with many collectors, he didn't purposefully set out to start a collection of barf bags. It happened when he asked a friend's daughter to pick up any items that contained the logo or name of the plane she was flying on. The airline was rumored to be going out of business, so he wanted to collect whatever he could before its demise. One of the articles he received was a barf bag. From that first bag a whole collection grew.

NO-COST AND LOW-COST COLLECTIBLE IDEAS

Starting a collection doesn't have to cost a lot of money. Here are some additional ideas that cost very little, or nothing at all. Most of these collections are for fun and not profit, but you never know when the next big fad could hit.

- **Arrowheads:** In most places in America that were once inhabited by Native Americans, you can find arrowheads left from various tribes. Actually, most arrowheads aren't arrowheads at all. They were originally spear points, knife blades, and various other cutting tools. The best place to look for arrowheads is near water, where tribes may have settled. Freshly tilled farmland is also a plentiful source, but be sure to get permission from the owner of the land before you start hunting!

- **Buttons:** Plain or fancy, buttons can be a fun and creative collection. Look for unusual shapes, such as fruit, stars, hearts, or animals. Or hunt out buttons with brightly colored stones. Then display them in glass jars on a windowsill, or make pictures using your most unusual buttons. You may want to sew or glue them on a fabric-covered board. You can find buttons at garage sales and flea markets. Don't pass up your mother's sewing box, either. Just ask her first what you may have.

- **Shells:** If you live near an ocean or even a river or a lake, you can find all kinds of interesting shells. (Ask friends and family members

49

to bring you some the next time they visit the beach.) You can find inexpensive shells in gift or craft shops and at flea markets.

● **Newspapers:** They're cheap, easy to find, and filled with lots of great information, which is why you may want to collect newspapers. Save articles about significant events, or chronicle life in your city or town. Someday the collection will be a treasured reminder of your times growing up. Paste individual articles in a scrapbook. The whole paper is most valuable with all its sections intact. Store each newspaper in a plastic bag in a cool, dry place.

● **Erasers:** You probably use them every day at school. So dig into your pencil bag and start collecting. Erasers come in a variety of colors and shapes. But remember, they're only valuable if they have not been used. While you're at it, expand your collection to include unusual pencils and pencil sharpeners. Call it your school supply collection!

● **A holiday collection:** Who says Christmas comes only once a year? If you start a collection based on Christmas decorations like Santas, snow people, and glass balls, it can be Christmas every day, or at least feel like it. To keep your collecting costs down, look for these collectibles at garage sales, or at

after-holiday sales, when prices are marked way down. If Christmas isn't your favorite holiday, the calendar is filled with others—Hanukkah, Valentine's Day, St. Patrick's Day, Easter, and Halloween, for example. Choose your favorite.

License plates: While traveling by car, you've probably played the license plate game where you try to spot different plates. Well, now try collecting old license plates from as many different states and countries as you can. It may sound weird, but a lot of people do it. There's even an organization for collectors, The National License Plate Collectors of America. Yard sales, rummage sales, and garage sales are the best places to look for old license plates. For more information, contact the Automobile License Collectors Association of America at:

> Automobile License Collectors Association
> c/o Gary Brent Kincade, Secretary-Treasurer
> P.O. Box 7
> Horner, WV 26372

Cereal boxes: The box your favorite breakfast cereal comes in can be a collector's item. Boxes that contain pictures of major celebrities are especially popular. Even the value of relatively recent boxes is rising. A Ralston box with a picture of the Addam's Family, printed in 1991, is already worth $15. Wheaties boxes picturing sports celebrities are very popular.

Pins: Nowadays, you can find all kinds of collector pins—Olympic pins, novelty pins, souvenir pins, even fast-food chains have offered pins.

KIDCOLLECTOR TIP #5

If you collect cereal boxes, don't tear a box up for the front picture! Collectors want the whole box. If storage is a problem, carefully loosen all the glued flaps and fold the box flat.

Collecting pins can be a fun way to remember special events or places you've visited. Most pins cost between $1 and $3. They're easy to display, too. Stick them to a bulletin board or pin them down a long ribbon.

Baseball caps: Baseball caps can get expensive in some retail and athletic stores. However, if you're patient in your collecting, you'll come across companies who give away caps for promotions, as well as those hats you get for any sports team you or your siblings are associated with.

Stickers: There are many possibilities for sticker-collecting. With a variety of shapes and sizes, stickers can be funny, sweet, or scary. Some even feature pictures of your favorite TV or movie stars. Current favorites among collectors are stickers from the Lisa Frank Studios. Fans of the Lisa Frank stickers love the bright colors and adorable creatures. Stickers can cost between $1 to $4 for a sheet of 10 to 20. You can get lots of stickers free, too, from the dentist, school book clubs, inside magazines, and at restaurants. Put the whole page of stickers inside a plastic sheet protector (you can get them from an office supply store). Then put the sheet protectors in a notebook that you can decorate with extra stickers.

GETTING STARTED

"I found lots of information about teddy bear collecting at the library. There was a book about old bears that I liked a lot. I even found a book on how to make a teddy bear."

Megan, age 12

You've decided what you want to collect. You have the space set aside and a little cash from those extra jobs you've done around the house. Now, where do you go from here? First, take some time to learn more about your collectible— especially its history and the best places to look for it. That will require a little detective work. See some ideas on the following pages for tracking down background information.

Head to the Library

You'll find books on specific categories of collecting, like stamps and baseball cards, at your local library. Since not every collection will have

its own book, you may have to look for titles that cover a variety of collectibles. One source is *Maloney's Antiques & Collectibles Resource Directory* (1993, Antique Trader), which has information on 10,000 resources for 2,600 categories of collectibles. If your library doesn't have it, search for other books under the category of "collections." Next, pore through the magazine section. Periodical indexes will help you pinpoint specific articles on your favorite collectibles.

CHECK IT OUT!

A terrific resource is *Warman's Americana & Collectibles*, published in 1993. It's packed with information on hundreds of collectibles, including some history about the collectible, a list of periodicals and price guides, and lists of clubs and museums. Check for the book in your local library.

Go Shopping

It's time to "browse" and find out what's available. Collectibles can be found at department stores, discount stores, and gift shops. Some specialty shops deal with only one type of collectible, such as comic books, stamps, or trading cards. Check your phone book for a shop near you. Flea markets and yard sales can be among the best places to begin looking, because the junk that someone else wants to get rid of cheaply could be that treasure you've been searching for!

Ask Questions

Like a good detective, ask questions of everyone you meet on your collectible search. You'll find that people love to talk about their favorite collection. They will tell you things you need to know and where to go in your community to search for bargains. Talk to shop owners, librarians, neighbors, and friends and tell them you're interested in starting a collection. Even if the people you're talking to aren't collectors themselves, they might know someone who is.

My KidCollection

"I collect <u>Star Wars</u> cards. I was ten when my friend bought me a pack of cards. My friends Taylor, Tyler, and Jeff also collect. I buy cards usually at the grocery store, but I also like to trade with my friends. It saves me money."

MICHAEL, AGE 11

55

FOR MORE INFORMATION

A *good way to learn more information about your favorite collectible is to join a collectors' club and read collectors' magazines and price guides. These sources will have everything to get you on the road to becoming a successful collector.*

CLUBS

There is a club or organization for most types of collections. These clubs offer valuable information that can't be found anyplace else. Sometimes they even have special discounts for their members at stores selling the collectibles. Almost all of them send out newsletters with the latest news. Many clubs have local or regional meetings so you can meet other collectors and share information.

MAGAZINES

Some magazines are published by national companies and cover a specific type of collectible, like comic books or stamps. There are also newsletters and small publications put out by collectors who want to reach others with the same interest. Check *Warman's Americana & Collectibles* for names and addresses. A few magazines cover many collectibles, such as *Collector's Mart Magazine* and *Today's Collector.* You may find these magazines at your local library, or check larger newsstands for copies.

PRICE GUIDES

A price guide tells you the current prices for particular items. The most common collectibles have their own price guides. Sometimes the prices listed are estimates of what a particular collectible might sell for. Sometimes they're based on reported sales. Most major categories of collectibles have several price guides. To really know your collectible, you should refer to as many different price guides as you can.

COLLECTING TIME IN A BOX

A collection doesn't always have to be about things—it can be about memories. With a few select pieces of memorabilia and a small box, you can create your own time capsule. Think of it as a way of preserving and recording your own history. A time capsule collection can commemorate a special day, such as a birthday or a family reunion, or it can chronicle an ordinary day in your life.

"A DAY IN THE Life OF THE JohNSONS"

■ First, collect things for your time capsule. These can be items from special events, such as party napkins, dinner menus, printed announcements or invitations, or candles from a birthday cake. Remember to include lots of snapshots. For a "day in the life of" time capsule, collect things you find around your house—the front page of a newspaper, that "A" math test you're so proud of, a T-shirt with a memorable saying, your dog's old license tags, or anything else you can think of.

■ Then, make tags to attach to each object. Cut 2" x 4" pieces out of lightweight cardboard. Write the date and any important information

on the tag. (Say, for a T-shirt, include how old you are and where you got it.) Use a hole puncher to make a hole in the tag and thread a piece of string through it. Tie it to your memento or use a safety pin to fasten it.

■ Next, put everything in a cardboard box and seal it shut with tape. With a marker, write down a title and the date, such as "Melinda's tenth birthday" or "A Day in the Life of the Johnsons, December 3, 1997."

■ Find a place in your house to store your time capsule, such as the basement, the attic, or the back of your closet.

■ In a few years (you determine when) open up your box. Your time capsule will tell the story of one special moment in your life. And who knows, you may have a box full of valuable collectibles.

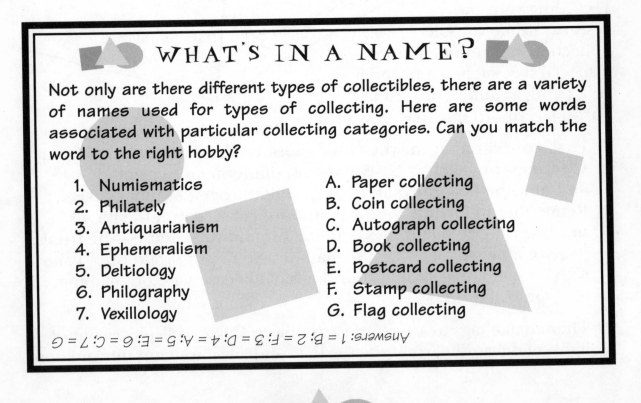

WHAT'S IN A NAME?

Not only are there different types of collectibles, there are a variety of names used for types of collecting. Here are some words associated with particular collecting categories. Can you match the word to the right hobby?

1. Numismatics
2. Philately
3. Antiquarianism
4. Ephemeralism
5. Deltiology
6. Philography
7. Vexillology

A. Paper collecting
B. Coin collecting
C. Autograph collecting
D. Book collecting
E. Postcard collecting
F. Stamp collecting
G. Flag collecting

Answers: 1 = B; 2 = F; 3 = D; 4 = A; 5 = E; 6 = C; 7 = G

JOIN THE CLUB

It seems as if there's a collectors' club for just about every collectible! If you're interested in any of the clubs below, request information about joining. It may speed your response if you send a SASE (self-addressed, stamped envelope).

PEN & PENCIL COLLECTIBLES
American Pencil Collectors
222 S. Milwood
Wichita, KS 67213

COOKIE CUTTERS
Cookie Cutter Collector Club
1167 Teal Road, SW
Dellroy, OH 44620

FROG-RELATED COLLECTIBLES
The Frog Pond
P.O. Box 193
Beech Grove, IN 46107

GI JOE ACTION FIGURES & ACCESSORIES
GI Joe Collectors Club
150 S. Glenoaks Blvd.
Burbank, CA 91510

MCDONALD'S PREMIUMS & GIVEAWAYS
McDonald's Collectors Club
2315 Ross Dr.
Stow, OH 44224

KEYS
Key Collectors International
P.O. Box 9397
Phoenix, AZ 85068

DISNEY CARTOON CHARACTER–RELATED COLLECTIBLES
National Fantasy Club for Disneyana
P.O. Box 19212
Irvine, CA 91521

SODA POP CANS
National Pop Can Collectors
1124 Tyler St.
Fairfield, CA 94533

TOOTHPICK HOLDERS & DISPENSERS
National Toothpick Holder Collectors Society
P.O. Box 246
Sawyer, MI 49125

CHILDREN'S TOY DISH SETS
Toy Dish Collectors
P.O. Box 351
Camilius, NY 13031

A Puzzling Collection

Jerry Slocum likes puzzles. He REALLY likes puzzles—so much so, he's built a house to store and display his collection of over 18,000 puzzles. These are not your ordinary jigsaw puzzles. Jerry specializes in mechanical and dexterity puzzles. Some are interlocking puzzles that boggle the mind. Others are puzzles requiring the player to roll, throw, or slide a piece of it. Still others are sequential-movement puzzles with pieces that move in a precise order. This lifelong obsession started when he was eight years old, and his parents gave him an interlocking plastic key-chain puzzle from the 1939 New York World's Fair.

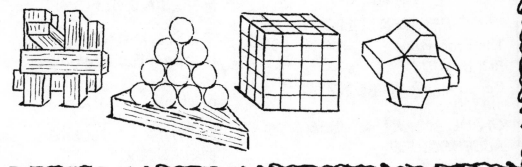

CHAPTER 5

PUTTING YOUR COLLECTION TOGETHER

"My dad gave me his old marbles from when he was a kid. Now I collect them, too. I can buy new marbles in the store, but I like to find old ones at yard sales. My favorites are the ones with swirls."

Adam, age 9

No two collections are ever the same. A collector who wants to complete a collection—or make room for more pieces—can trade, buy, sell, and resell to other collectors. Here's the scoop on how it's done.

BUYING COLLECTIBLES

Part of the fun of collecting is getting creative on your search for collectibles. Here are a few places to check out:

Specialty Stores

For some types of collecting, you'll find specific stores devoted to one type of collection, such as comic book shops, sport memorabilia shops, and so on. Whatever you find, expect to pay full retail prices. Don't miss these other stores: Discount stores, department stores, and even grocery stores are sources to find items to add to your collection.

Rummage Sales

Almost every weekend in a neighborhood near you, people clean out their closets and basements and put unwanted stuff up for sale. These

neighborhood sales go by different names—garage sales, yard sales, basement sales. These are some of the best places to find collectibles at cheap prices.

Flea Markets and Swap Meets

Almost every town and city has a flea market or a swap meet, where all sorts of individuals come to sell their new or used products. You'll find everything from sophisticated Oriental rugs to dime-store plastic gadgets. In cold weather areas, flea markets and swap meets may only be held in the summer, or may be held inside big buildings. Some swap meets charge an admission fee.

Catalogs and Mail Order

Shopping by mail is easy—the information is right in front of you. All types of collectibles can be found in mail-order catalogs. The downside of ordering from a catalog is that you don't see in person what you're buying. It's best to make sure that the catalog you're ordering from has a good return policy. You should find that information in the ordering section of the catalog. The best source for finding catalogs is

KIDCOLLECTOR TIP #6

When you go to rummage sales and flea markets, remember to look under other items. The collectible could be stuck under a pile of something else. Also, ask the person who's running the sale if they have what you're looking for. After all, there may be items that haven't been put out yet.

in a magazine that features your favorite collectible. Sometimes you may have to pay for the catalog. When you order something from a catalog, you'll probably have to get your parents to help, because most catalog sales require a credit card. You can also get money orders from the Post Office, or cashier's checks from the bank, to pay for your purchases. But never, never send cash!

Auctions

Auction houses specialize in different types of merchandise. Some sell nothing but fine antiques, while others sell a little of everything.

HOW TO STRIKE A BARGAIN

When you go to a retail store, you expect to pay the marked prices. But it's a different story when you shop at rummage sales, flea markets, and swap meets—bargaining is expected. Follow these helpful hints below to learn how!

- Don't be afraid to ask for a lower price. You might think you're insulting the sellers, but they often ask for a higher price than they expect to get. It's fairly common to get at least 10 percent off the asking price. One approach that works is to ask "Is that your best price?" or "Can you do better?"

- Ask vendors about their volume discounts. Most vendors do offer a price break if you buy so many items or spend a certain amount of money.

Auctions can also be a treasure trove of collectibles. If you see an auction advertised, the ad will probably say what's for sale. The auction house is made up of the people who hold the auction. The actual auction can be held in different locations. Check the ad for phone numbers or look under *Auctions* in the Yellow Pages of your telephone directory. Auctions are different from other sales because people bid against each other to buy merchandise. So the price you pay for an item will depend on how much someone else is willing to pay.

An auctioneer starts the process and keeps track of each bid (the price the buyer offers). Sometimes auctions go very fast, and it's hard to know what's going on. Kids can go to an auction, but usually they are not allowed to bid. If you are interested in buying collectibles at an auction, be sure to bring along an adult. The best tips for buying at an auction are to examine the items you want before the sale, understand the rules of the auction, and don't get caught up in the frenzy of bidding. Keep your head and ask the adult to bid only what you think the item is worth.

A Collectors' Show or Convention

Each year thousands of collectors meet to swap and sell sports cards, stamps, comics, models, and other collectibles. These shows include lots of vendors who buy, sell, and trade the collectibles you may want. Big shows are usually held in the convention halls of large cities. But smaller shows are scheduled in both towns and cities, sometimes even in local malls. The best place to find dates for collector shows or

KIDCOLLECTOR TIP #7

You may have to go no farther than your own home to start a collection. If you're interested in a key collection, check with your parents for extra keys they may no longer need. If old hats are your passion, check with your grandparents and aunts and uncles. You never know what treasure trove of stuff they may have in their attics.

conventions is in magazines and newsletters on the specific type of collecting. Keep an eye on the local newspaper, too. Conventions of this sort are usually heavily advertised.

My KidCollection

"I collect glass turtles because when I was five I had a real pet turtle. Turtles are so neat I wanted to have more, just not real ones. I have ten turtles, and I put them up on the shelves in my bedroom so I can see them."

ALAN, AGE 12

Other Collectors

One of the best sources to find your favorite collectible may be through other collectors. Some people may have to make way for new items in their collection by selling off old ones. Check the classified section of your local newspaper for advertisements. Also check with a local group or club for your favorite collectible.

TRADING COLLECTIBLES

You'll save money when you find trading partners. You've probably already done some trading, like that banana-and-bologna sandwich in exchange for an oatmeal-raisin cookie from your friend at lunch. Or an extra piece of gum for half of a candy bar from your little brother. Trading is simply exchanging something you don't want or need for something that you do want. For the how-tos, read on.

1. **Determine what you can trade.** Go through your collection and write down any duplicates of an item. Decide what you no longer need or want. Make a list. You may find you have more things to get rid of than you first thought.

2. **Figure out its value.** Now that you know what you want to trade, figure out what each item is worth. Do your research, and read price guides, look through catalogs, and check the going prices at local

collectible stores or with other collectors. Remember, determining the value of what you're trading is important. You don't want to trade a $10 sports card for one worth only $2.

3. **Find trading partners.** Start with your own friends. More than likely your friends will have the same interests as you. Maybe even the same collection. And sometimes your friends might have something you want to collect that they think isn't important. As you get more into collecting, you might find a club, a group, or just other collectors who want to trade their duplicate collectibles.

SELLING COLLECTIBLES

You might think that after spending a great deal of time putting your collection together, you'd never want to sell it. But there are lots of reasons to sell. Sometimes you may want to make room for more collectibles. Or you might want to devote your energies to another hobby. Search out the two types of people who will be most excited to buy your collections: dealers and collectors.

Dealers

A dealer buys your collectibles to sell to other collectors. As a result, he won't want to pay you as much as he can charge for them because a dealer must make a profit to stay in business. In other words, the profit

is the difference between what a dealer pays for a collectible and what he can sell it for. The advantage of selling your collection—or a piece of it—to a dealer is that you won't have to go through the trouble of finding a buyer. Weigh the pros and cons of selling to a dealer or selling pieces yourself and decide what makes the most sense for your situation.

Other Collectors

Selling to other collectors allows you to sell your pieces for the going price. Plus, you will know your collectible is going to someone who cares for the item as much as you do. The key is finding the collector to sell to, which usually means advertising. Take advantage of free advertising—use supermarket bulletin boards, flyers, or best of all, word of mouth. Let other collectors know what you are selling. You may also want to place an ad in the newspaper, but it will cost you some money.

SHOPPING TIPS

The next time you go collection shopping, keep these tips in mind.

- **Plan ahead.** Before you shop, check price guides to know the approximate

My KidCollection

"I collect Beanie Babies. I just started my collection about three weeks ago. I have friends who collect Beanie Babies, too. I only have about five Beanie Babies, but I like what I collect."

NICOLE, AGE 11

prices of the items you'll be buying.

■ **Be early.** If your shopping trip includes garage sales or flea markets, be there when they open. Often the best deals are sold early. Also, you want to allow yourself plenty of time to carefully inspect the items you're interested in buying.

■ **Make notes.** If you're not going to buy immediately, make notes about what you like. Include where you saw it and how much it was. When you've been shopping all day, it's easy to forget what you've seen at one place.

My KidCollection

"I collect the toys in Happy Meals. My collection got started when I was about nine. I add more toys to my collection every time I go to McDonald's. If I get two of the same thing, I never open the second one. I save it in the package."

CARYN, AGE 11

- **Set spending limits.** When you find the "perfect" piece for your collection, you may talk yourself into spending more than you planned. Sticking to your spending limits will save you money in the long run to buy what you really want.

- **Be prepared.** If what you like to collect is big and bulky, or small and fragile, always bring along something you can take your purchase home in. Bring cardboard boxes and plenty of newspaper to wrap up any breakable purchases.

- **Don't get discouraged.** If you don't get what you want at a particular event, be assured that there will be others.

KIDCOLLECTOR TIP #8

Let everyone know you're starting a collection so they can "surprise" you on your birthday and other gift-giving occasions.

ORGANIZING YOUR COLLECTION

"I collect teddy bears in different costumes. I got started when my mom brought me home one when I was about seven years old. I bought wooden stands to put them on. I keep my bears in stands to show off their costumes."

Staci, age 11

I t doesn't take long for your collection to fill every nook and cranny of your bedroom—maybe even the rest of the house.

Before long, you won't know what you have, much less where it is. If your collection is important to you, then you have to take care of it. It's time to organize!

Keep a Record

List each object in your collection. You may think it's silly to have a list of only four or five things, but you'll be happy you started a list once your collection grows. Next to each entry include when you got it,

ITEM #	MY SANTA Collectibles DESCRIPTION	Date Received	Price	Location
01	Stuffed SANTA with LINEN outfit	christmas '94	Gift from JODY	Canada
02	Santa in Snow Shake Ball	1/15/95	$40.00 (marked at 50%)	christmas shop, Aspen Colorado
03	Santa Stocking, BLUE	10/13/96	$10.00	THE HOLIDAY Store Los Angeles
04	Musical Santa play "we wish you A merry christmas"	CHRISTMAS 1997	Gift from Mom & Dad	?
05				
06				

where you bought it (or who gave it to you), and how much you spent on it. You can keep your collection record in a notebook, card file, or a database program on your computer. (Check out the sample record sheet below.)

Label It

Label your collectibles by numbers to track down information on each one quickly. Use small, removable self-adhesive stickers from a stationery store. Give your collectible a number on your record sheet (see below), and write the same number on the label. Place the label on the bottom of your collectible. If you can't put a sticker on the collectible, you might be able to put a label next to the item or attach the label with string.

KIDCOLLECTOR RECORD

Copy this list to create your own records.

ITEM #	DESCRIPTION	DATE RECEIVED	PRICE	LOCATION
01	brown bear wearing sailor's uniform	2/15/97	$9	Pier 39, San Francisco
02	yellow bear wearing cowboy hat	9/19/97	$7.50	Jackson Hole, Wyoming

Take Pictures

To have an accurate record of your
collection, you should also take a
photograph of each object.
This is especially important if
your collection is valuable, for
instance coins or antique dolls.
A photograph of your collectibles
is also good to have on hand when
you want to sell. With a picture, you
won't have to bring your whole
collection and take a chance of
losing it. If you don't have your own
camera, try to borrow one. When
you get prints back, keep them
with your record. Keep both your
records and pictures in a safe fire-proof box.

Insure It

Unless your
collection is worth
$1,000 or more, you
and your parents
probably won't
need to insure it
separately. That
doesn't mean
everyday, not-so-
extraordinary
collections aren't
insurable. Even if
each individual piece
of your collection
doesn't cost much, a

whole collection can add up in value. If your parents have a homeowner's insurance policy, your collection will probably be covered.

In the event something should happen to your collection, such as theft or fire, your records and pictures will show the insurance company the value of your collection. Make a copy of your records and give that, and your photographs, to your parents for safekeeping in a place outside your house, such as a safe-deposit box at the bank.

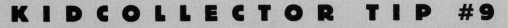

My KidCollection

"For my sports cards, I organize them by teams and put them in a trunk in my bedroom. I have about a thousand cards."

JOHN, AGE 12

DISPLAYING YOUR COLLECTIBLES

You've spent hours searching out your favorite collectibles. Now they're scattered all over your room. Everything is getting stepped on, trampled, or worse . . . forgotten. Here are some simple ideas to gather up your collections and show them off.

KIDCOLLECTOR TIP #9

If you're tight on space, try these ideas!

• Place a small mirror on a shelf behind your collectibles to make a smaller collection look like it has more pieces.

• You don't have to display your entire collection at one time. Rotate pieces every few weeks. It'll feel like you have a new collection each time.

Shelve It

If you are short on space in your room, look to the wall and add shelves. Check with your parents first. You'll need their permission and their help to hang the shelves. Check local building supply stores for materials. You can usually find prepackaged shelf units with all the hanging essentials. If you can't add shelves, think about freestanding bookcases. They come in a variety of sizes and finishes and can be found at local discount stores.

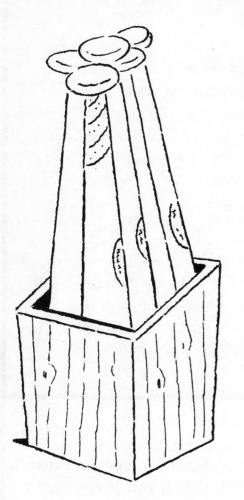

Contain It

Look for interesting containers at yard and garage sales. Glass jars are great for showing off small collectibles, like marbles and buttons. Large wicker baskets or wooden boxes can hold lots of big treasures, such as dolls or a collection of baseball bats.

My KidCollection

"I collect pigs. I got started when I was five and saw a pig in a store. Now it's my favorite animal to collect. I put them on a shelf so the bigger ones are in the back. And I dust them with a rag every two weeks."

RACHEL, AGE 11

Use It

While you're checking out yard sales for your favorite collectibles, look for old furniture to use as display units. Old benches and tables can hold everything from books to a collection of horse figures. A cradle is the perfect display spot for your collection of stuffed animals.

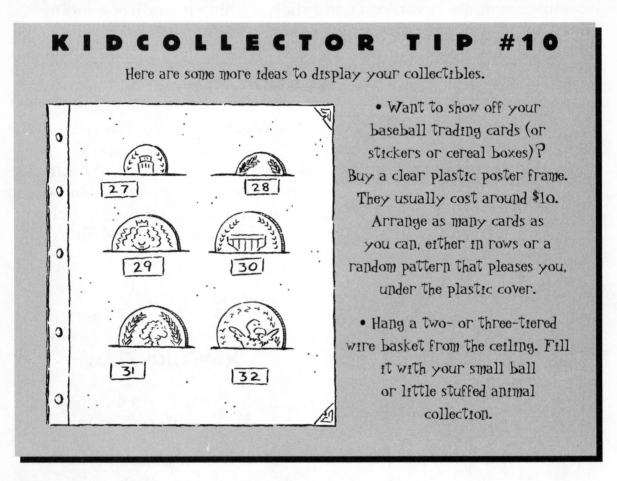

KIDCOLLECTOR TIP #10

Here are some more ideas to display your collectibles.

• Want to show off your baseball trading cards (or stickers or cereal boxes)? Buy a clear plastic poster frame. They usually cost around $10. Arrange as many cards as you can, either in rows or a random pattern that pleases you, under the plastic cover.

• Hang a two- or three-tiered wire basket from the ceiling. Fill it with your small ball or little stuffed animal collection.

PROTECTING COLLECTIBLES

You've collected, recorded, photographed, and built the perfect display for your favorite collectibles. But you're not finished yet. If you don't take extra care of your collectibles, they're likely to lose value or fall apart.

▲ **DO handle with care.** Whether your collectibles are fragile and expensive or tough and cheap, always handle them carefully. If the item is small, it should be held in a cupped hand. If it is large, support it with both hands.

▲ **DON'T leave it out in the sun.** Sunlight can be a real problem. It can fade the color of most collectibles (glass is generally the exception), or melt things (especially candles). It's best to keep your favorite things out of sunlight.

▲ **DO clean it.** You don't have to spend hours cleaning your collection. An occasional dusting will keep your collection in good condition.

▲ **DON'T get it wet.** If you spill water on your collectible, dry it immediately. Water left on almost any object can warp, rust, or peel its paint over time.

WEIRD AND WACKY COLLECTORS

It's Magic!

Did you ever watch a magician and wonder how he or she did all those cool tricks? Well, Ken Klosterman wondered that, too. At nine years old he developed a passion for magic when his uncle showed him a coin trick. Fifty years later this former professional magician collects magic memorabilia and displays it in his very own museum. The Salon de Magie, as he calls it, is built eight stories below his house in a former mining shaft. Complete with tunnels, secret passageways, and a 24-seat theater, the private museum is a historical tribute to magic. It is filled with magic collectibles through history—books, posters, marked decks, and critics' reviews of more than 5,000 magicians.

A FOREVER COLLECTION

Many collectors remember their childhoods through their collections. By becoming a KidCollector, you will be able to start building your memories now. Don't look at collecting as a hobby you'll do for a month or a year. Collecting for many becomes a lifelong journey of discovery. Many of the things you learn while building your collection will serve you well as you get older. Learning to sort and categorize is one part of it. Learning to shop well and bargain is another. Lastly, collecting is about learning to appreciate people and things. Happy collecting!

My KidCollection

"I collect flying pigs.
You don't find them many
places, and so far I only
have four. But I like
them, or at least the idea
of them, because if a
pig can fly, anything
is possible."

K.D., THE AUTHOR